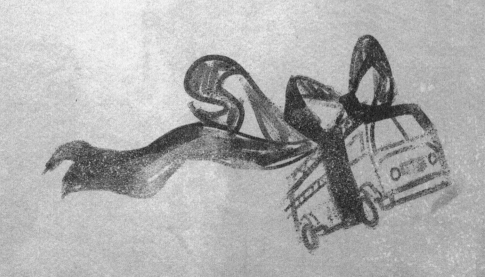

The Christmas Truck

Written by J. B. Blankenship

Illustrated by Cassandre Bolan

ISBN-13: 978-0-9907434-1-5 (bound).
ISBN-13: 978-0-9907434-0-8 (pbk).

The Christmas Truck is a work of fiction.
All characters are products of the author's imagination. Any similarities to real people, events, and incidents are purely coincidental.

Summary: When celebrating a special Christmas tradition things go awry and one family must work together to save Christmas for a child they have never met.

Key Words
[1.Seasonal – Juvenile Fiction. 2. Christmas – Juvenile Fiction.
3. Social Issues – Juvenile Fiction. 4. Gay and Lesbian – Juvenile Fiction.
5. Children's Ages 6-8.]

Ordering Information:
Quantity sales. Special discounts are available on quantity purchases by corporations, associations, and others. For details, contact the publisher at the address above or visit www.narragarden.com

Cover design by Cassandre Bolan and J.B. Blankenship.
Interior textures and page layout by Destini Richlin.
Text type set in St Nicholas font Copyright © 2014 by The Scriptorium, all rights reserved.

First American edition, September 2014

For anyone who needs a little Christmas magic
For my Mama, Papa, Big Brother, & Little Brother
And for my Monks
-J.B.

To
My family, for endlessly supporting me and my crazy ways
My husband, for dragging me out of my comfort zones and encouraging my weirdness
My son, who makes me smile everyday and inspired the kid in this book
And all the kids out there who feel like they are different.
-Cassandre Bolan

Christmas time is coming! I can feel it in the air.
My tummy starts to tingle 'cause it's Christmas everywhere.
Papa is in the kitchen baking chocolate Christmas treats,
while Dad is in the front yard hanging lights up on our street.

'We go down to the market to get our Christmas tree.
Outside it started snowing on Papa, Dad, and me.

Next we set the tree up in the window by the stair
and put on decorations with loving gentle care.
"The tree is nearly ready" I hear my Papa say.
"It's time to place the star and give thanks for Christmas Day!"

Now our tree is finished. It is perfect as can be.
Now we wait for Christmas; Papa, Dad, and me.

Christmas time is coming, I can see it in the sights.
Houses on our block are decked out in Christmas lights.
We drive around the town, Papa, Dad, and me,
and search for Christmas visions and the town square Christmas tree.

The tree is full of wishes with names of girls and boys.
They come from different families who don't have many toys.
Daddy lifts me up and Papa's voice rings clear,
"It's time to pick our wish and spread some Christmas cheer!"

We find the perfect wish. The name is Michael Clay.
And written on the wish are things for Christmas Day.
"I would like a fire truck, a shirt and socks and shoes,
and Mama says that gloves are things that I can use."

When I finish reading, my Papa looks at me;
"Do you understand the meaning of this tree?"
My tummy starts to rumble. I feel for Michael Clay.
"Yes," I tell my parents, "it's the spirit of Christmas Day."

Daddy and my Papa help me fill the list.
Then we box and wrap them up and seal them with a kiss.
We take the gifts for Michael and put them by our tree,
and on the cards I write "from Papa, Dad, and me."

Christmas time is coming. It's just a day away.
Grandma and my grandpa bring the turkey on a tray.

My uncle and my auntie, they come and visit too.
Our Christmas Eve tradition is to eat an oyster stew.

When we all are eating we hear a sudden sound.

A CRASH.

A BANG.

"Something's wrong!" We all just look around.

The Christmas tree had fallen and had broken into two.
The bottom in the presents and the top went in the stew!
Our eyes are all wide open as we gaze at such a sight.
'Who thought a big disaster could happen Christmas Night?

We inspect every present and each one is okay,
except for one, the fire truck, the gift for Michael Clay!
"That was his special present. From Papa, Dad, and me!
His Christmas is now ruined because of our broke tree!"

And then my grandma says to me, "I have a plan for you.
Do you remember what I was? What I used to do?"
My grandma takes her phone out and makes a friendly call.
She used to be the fire chief, beloved by one and all.
And in a few short moments, I hear a distant sound.
A fire truck pulls up! A new present we have found!

Papa grabs the broken tree and ties it to the truck.
We cheer him on and laugh a lot, thankful for our luck!
We load all of the presents into a Christmas sack.
Grandma takes the driver's seat, and we all take the back.
With the truck all decked out, we set out in the night.
To Michael's house we drive ourselves. We are a Christmas sight!

We pull into his driveway. Our lights are all ablaze.
Michael and his mom come out. They look at us, amazed!
"Merry Christmas, Michael!" I announce with Christmas glee.
"Here's a shiny fire truck. From Papa, Dad, and me!"

'We hand out all the presents, our Christmas spirit strong.
And then with cheer, we all join hands and sing a Christmas song.
Christmas time is here. I can feel it in the air.
The joy of giving presents has no joy that can compare.

The season is for giving! You don't have to have a tree!
Merry Christmas everyone from Papa, Dad, and Me!

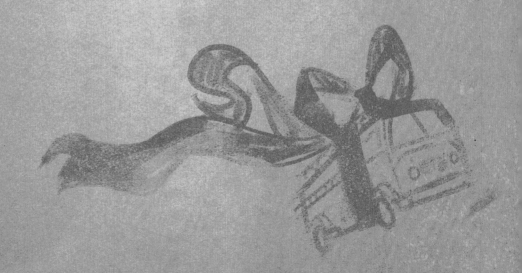

About the Author
When not writing stories or in search of adventure, J.B. Blankenship and his dog, Cosi Fan Tutte, volunteer with a local literacy organization teaching inner city youth. He lives in Chicago, Illinois and frequently snacks on green apples, peanut butter, and Swiss cheese.

About the Illustrator
Cassandre Bolan is a world-traveling, jasmine tea-drinking, mismatched sock-wearing illustrator who believes in painting what you believe. Her work spans trading cards, teen/adult book covers, concept art, and now children's books, but all of them have a common theme: we all have more similarities than we do differences. To see more of her work visit: www.cassandrebolan.com.

CPSIA information can be obtained at www.ICGtesting.com
Printed in the USA
LVOW01*0404131114

413467LV00019B/46/P